59786

JOKES TO TELL YOUR DAD

Library of Congress Catalog-in-Publication Data
Woodworth, Viki
Jokes to Tell Your Dad / Compiled and illustrated by Viki Woodworth.
p. cm.
Summary: Presents a collection of jokes featuring fathers and their offspring.

ISBN 1-56766-098-3
1. Wit and humor, Juvenile
[1. Jokes 2. Father and child—Wit and humor.]
I. Title.
PN8163.W683 1995   93-15443
816'.5402–dc20   CIP/AC

JOKES
TO TELL
YOUR DAD

Compiled and Illustrated by
Viki Woodworth

THE CHILD'S WORLD

Dad: Why are you playing pool with that vegetable?
Bill: It's a cue-cumber.

Dad: Why are you carrying a dictionary in your pocket?
Son: To be a smartypants.

Dad: Son, I heard you missed school yesterday.
Son: No, I didn't miss it in the least.

Dad: I'm going to give you a piece of my mind!
Daughter: Are you sure you can spare it?

Son: Dad, do you know the difference between the North and South Pole?
Dad: There's a world of difference.

Aaron: I just played basketball with a pig!
Dad: Oh, was it fun?
Aaron: No, all he did was hog the ball.

Dad: Does that dog have fleas?
Maryanne: No, just puppies.

Dad: There's a bull charging us!
Nora: Well, pay him!

Dad: Why are you putting in earplugs?
Diane: I'm going to a tennis match and there's always so much racket.

Son: That player smells.
Dad: Why?
Son: He hit a foul shot.

Peter: Do you know what sport cats like to play?
Dad: No, son, I don't.
Peter: Mice hockey.

Anne: Did you know there's a ghost on the football team?
Dad: No, really?
Anne: Sure, it's the team spirit.

Daughter: If I were a baby computer, do you know what I'd call you?
Dad: I don't know, what?
Daughter: Data.

Son: I just swallowed a quarter.
Dad: Oh no, are you choking?
Son: No, I'm serious.

Dad: Where does a witch go on vacation?
Son: Witch-ita, Kansas.

Dad: What does your pet shark read?
Don: Anything it can sink its teeth into.

Dad: What does a shark eat for breakfast?
Don: Ham and legs.

Dad: Why are you giving that paper to a cow?
Michelle: It's a moospaper.

Dad: Why are you feeding ice cream to the dog?
Mandy: Because they're pupsicles.

Don: How many people work in your office, Dad?
Dad: Not very many of them.

Joe: Dad, do you know the difference between a shoe and a steak?
Dad: No.
Joe: Good, then I'll fix dinner.

Son: I better take this colt to the doctor.
Dad: Why?
Son: It's hoarse.

Dad: What's the matter with your violin?
Son: I don't know, I think it has fiddle-ticks.

Dad: Why are you taking those clocks to the bank?
Daughter: I'm saving time.

Dad: Why are you laughing at those cows?
Christopher: They're from a funny farm.

Dad: Why are you laughing at that horse?
Taylor: It's a silly filly.

Son: What kind of water doesn't freeze?
Dad: I don't know, son.
Son: Hot water!

Heidi: Is the refrigerator running?
Dad: Yes.
Heidi: Gosh, you better catch it!

Dad: I swallowed a pen.
Daughter: What should I do?
Dad: Use a pencil.

Dad: I have ringing in my ears all the time.
Son: Why don't you get an unlisted ear?

59786

Zack: What has a horn and gives milk?
Dad: I don't know.
Zak: A milk truck.

Dad: Put the dog out.
Son: Is he on fire?

Dad: Did your class like your home video?
Son: They were glued to their seats.
Dad: Why, wouldn't they sit still?

Ed: I'm the most advanced in my class.
Dad: You are?
Ed: Yes, I sit in the front row.

Dad: Where should we take this sick horse?
Fran: To the horsepital.

Sandy: I just got my pet mouse some shoes.
Dad: What kind?
Sandy: Squeakers.

Mother Whale: What shall we name our baby?

Father Whale: How about Little Squirt?

Father Owl: What's your favorite subject in school?

Daughter Owl: Owl-gebra, of course.

Son Duck: What did you buy Mom for her birthday?

Dad Duck: A box of quackers.

Mother Werewolf: Where shall we stay on our vacation?

Father Werewolf: How about the Howl-iday Inn?

Father Vampire: Where did you deposit your money?

Son Vampire: In a bloodbank.

Mother Elephant: Sonny does so well in school.
Father Elephant: He has a lot of grey matter.

Father Duck: What should we watch on television?

Daughter Duck: How about a duckumentary?

Father Hamburger: Why are you so beat up?

Son Hamburger: I got into a meat brawl.

Father Mosquito: What's your favorite sport?

Daughter Mosquito: Skin-diving.

Daughter Fly: My report card stung me.

Father Fly: How?
Daughter Fly: It's full of B's.

Father Skunk: What did you deposit at the bank?

Son Skunk: Dollars and scents.

Son Sheep: Why are we so poor, Dad?
Father Sheep: Because we're always getting fleeced.

Daughter: That cow is from Hawaii.
Dad: How can you tell?
Daughter: It's wearing a moo-moo.

Daughter: That farmer doesn't need chickens.
Dad: Why not?
Daughter: He grows egg-plants.

Dad: Where does your hog keep its money?
Son: In a piggybank.

Dad: What shall we name our zebra?
Allie: Spot?

Dad: I just heard a mouse squeak.
Joyce: Did you expect it to say "hello"?

Tom: I put our cat in the copy machine!
Dad: What did you get?
Tom: Dupli-cats, of course!

Emily: What does the President have for a pet?
Dad: I don't know.
Emily: The Presidential Seal.

Anne: My dad's a lawyer.
Mac: What does he wear to work?
Anne: Law-suits, of course.

Jan: I thought you were a dentist in the army.
Dad: No, why?
Jan: You said you were a drill sergeant.

Son: Why did you quit being a carpenter?
Dad: Because I was chewing my nails.

Dad: Why did you bring me that glue?
Erin: To patch your splitting headache.

Stan: Dad, is that your Easter tie?
Dad: No, Son. Why?
Stan: It's got egg all over it.

DATE DUE

JE 12 '97	JE 18 '03		
JY 11	JE 26 03		
JE 15 '97	JY 3 '03		
JY 23 '98			
	JY 15 '03		
JE 16 '99	JY 31 '03		
AG 11 '99	JE 10 03		
MR 16 '00	OC 6 05		
JY 5 00	DE 12 05		
JY 21 00	AG 4 7		
JA 5 '01			
AP 7 '01			
JE 27 01			
JE 21 02			
JY 22 02			
FE 14 03			
MY 1 03			